GETTING STARTED

Let's begin by learning the basics of drawing the head of anime's most popular action characters.

THE CHARACTER LINEUP

When drawing new action characters, think about which elements you want to include in your fighting teams. You'll want a well-rounded action team and a few distinct villains to stir up trouble. Some of the most popular character types are shown below, but this is just a starting point.

ACTION
GIRL

ACTION
BOY

DARK
VILLAIN

TEEN
ENEMY

GROUP
LEADER

ACTION BOY

This young hero is a star of action manga. He fights every type of bad guy, even monsters. He is often surprisingly young for a character with so much riding on his victory, but making him look slightly underpowered is a surefire way to get the readers' attention, because it leads them to ask, "How in the world is he going to survive the match?!" But of course he will. He'll get knocked down a few times, then gather all the strength he can muster and attack with blinding fury.

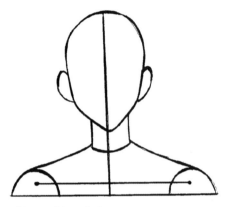

Vertical line helps create symmetry

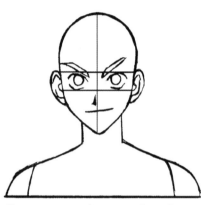

Eyes are spaced one eye-length apart

Hair flows out in all directions from origin of part

FROM ROUGH SKETCH TO FINISHED ART

Generally, a manga artist first blocks out a scene in pencil, then refines it to create a final pencil drawing. The inking is done by hand, right over the pencil lines. Most manga graphic novels are printed in gray tones, which can be created on a computer or shaded by hand. Anime (animated manga) is usually in color.

Soft face

FRONT VIEW

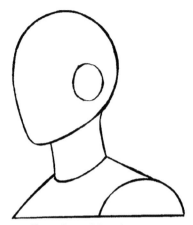

Egg-shaped head

Huge amount of hair falls in front of face

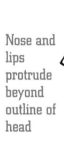 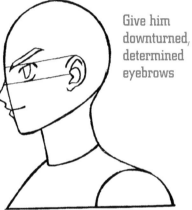

Nose and lips protrude beyond outline of head

Give him downturned, determined eyebrows

PROFILE

Notice how the action boy's slight build doesn't fill out his oversized jacket.

ACTION GIRL

This youthful character can fight alongside the young action hero or take on a few enemies on her own. Her slight build, wide eyes, and perky attitude may cause some evildoers to underestimate her. That would be a mistake. What she may lack in size, she makes up for in spunk, ingenuity, and fighting skill.

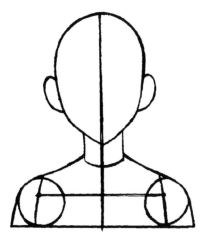

Thin neck

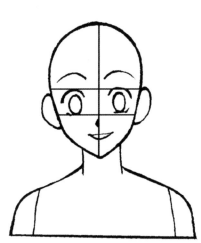

Tiny nose and mouth

Twin ponytails are a cute, young look.

FRONT VIEW

Young characters like this girl usually have lots of hair surrounding the head.

Bright eyes—eyebrows placed far above eyes in a high arch...

...and upper eyelids don't cover irises.

Ribbons in hair

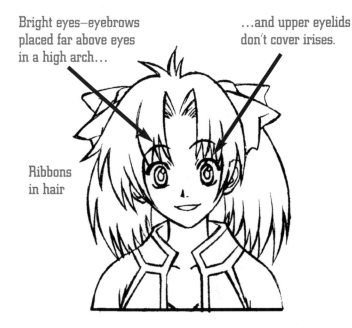

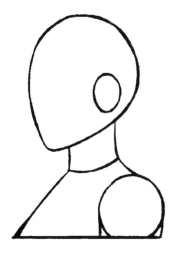

Jaw is round and soft looking

Features grouped low on face

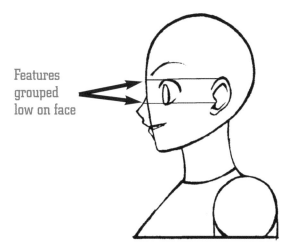

PROFILE

Darken top eyelid.

Her hairstyle is very full in back (and in front, too).

DRAWING EYES FOR ACTION CHARACTERS

How do you get good at drawing eyes? By drawing eyes! Let's focus on the eyes of teens—some of the most popular characters in action anime.

Be sure to vary the thickness of your line. Upper eyelids are always darker than lower eyelids. Remember to get the eyebrows into the act, too!

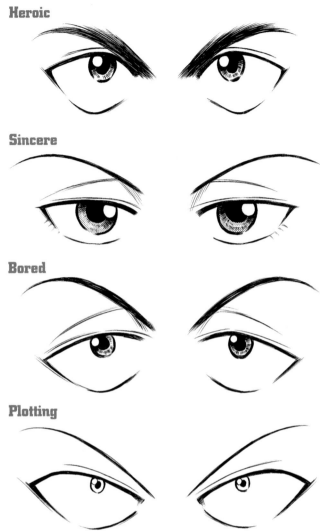

Heroic

Sincere

Bored

Plotting

Scared

YOUNG TEEN BOY

This very popular character type ranges in age from about 12 to 15. He's usually portrayed as earnest, sincere, and fiercely determined. But he lacks guile and is vulnerable to the double-dealing ways of villains. His pupils are normally large and round—a sign of honesty. But even he can have a bad thought flash across his eyes, which will result in beady pupils.

YOUNG TEEN GIRL

When you draw girls' eyes, think of dark eyelids and thick eyelashes that flare up at the ends. That's where the emphasis needs to be.

Calm

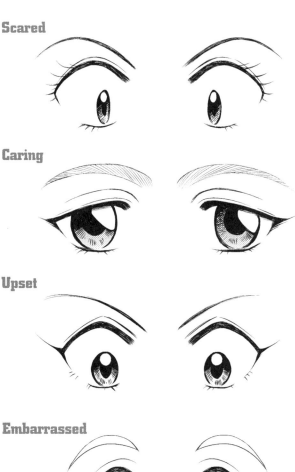

Scared

Caring

Upset

Embarrassed

THESE EYES ARE TRUE BLUE

This character is a loyal friend, one you want to have on your side when treachery is around every corner. She is often used to give the reader an "emotional cue." What does that mean? Here's an example: Suppose a powerful bad guy challenges our teen boy to a fight. When he naturally accepts, the girl freaks out. Why? Because she knows that the boy can't win—the enemy is too powerful. She begs him not to go ahead with the fight. The girl is giving the reader a cue that the fight is going to be extremely dangerous for our young hero. In this way, she helps build anticipation and heightens suspense.

CRAAAAZY EYES

Part of the fun of drawing evil characters is that you get to invent crazier eye types than when drawing the good guys, who have to look noble and honest. Completely blank eyeballs, pinpoint pupils, and eye patches are just a few surefire ways to make a character look creepy or wicked.

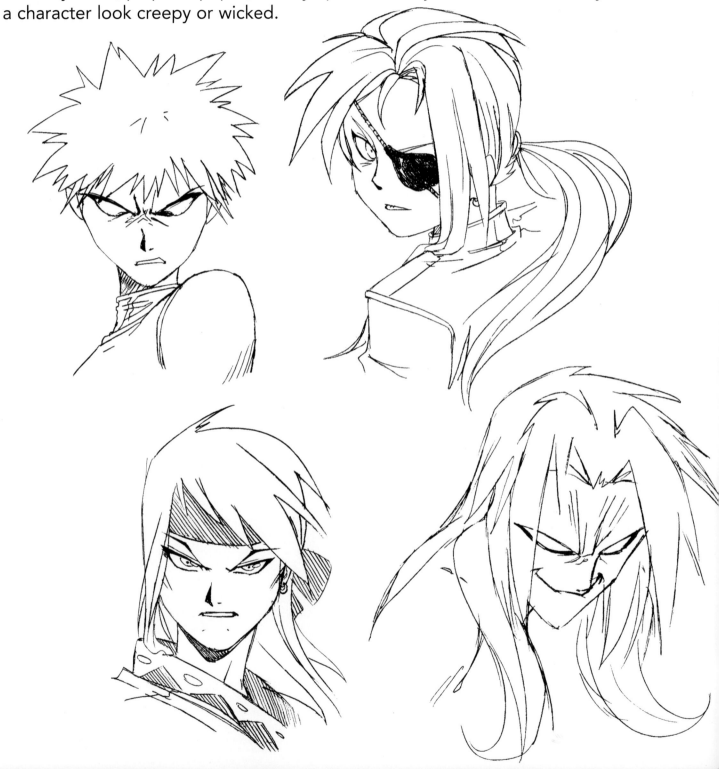

INTENSE EXPRESSIONS

Action is intense. There's usually a lot at stake—sometimes even life and death. The characters' expressions need to communicate this intensity to the reader. Use a liberal amount of shading just under the eyes to convey a face that is flushed with anger and emotion. Let the hair get shaggy and wild. And really work those eyebrows so that they push down at the bridge of the nose. Where applicable, grit the teeth—a sign of extreme emotion and distress.

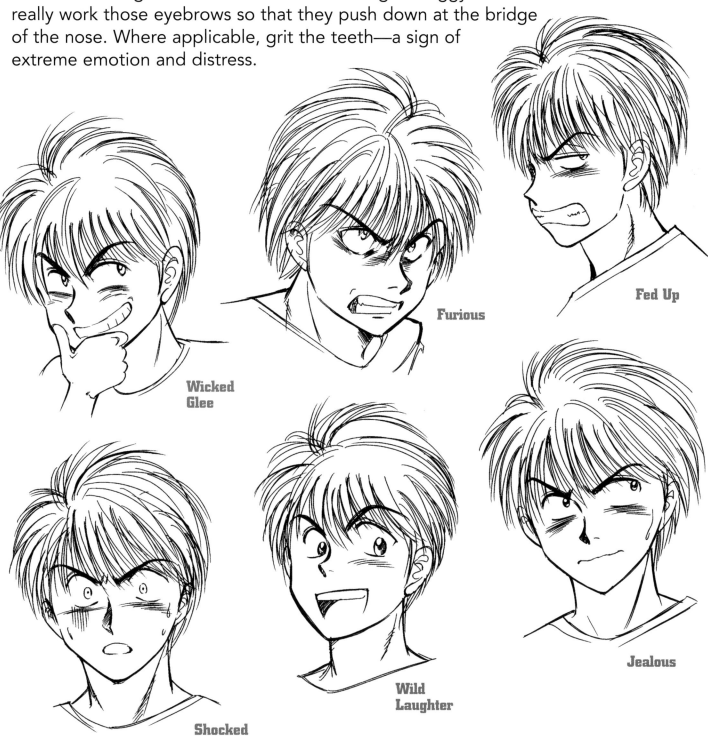

Wicked Glee

Furious

Fed Up

Shocked

Wild Laughter

Jealous

BRAVE FIGHTER KID

The fighter kid has a medium build. He's not overly muscular, but he's not skinny either. He's completely average—and that's the point of anime. Instead of super-powered heroes, regular guys and gals save the day. They're ordinary people doing extraordinary things, making it easy for us to relate to them. They don't need capes or superpowers, just guts and a fighting spirit.

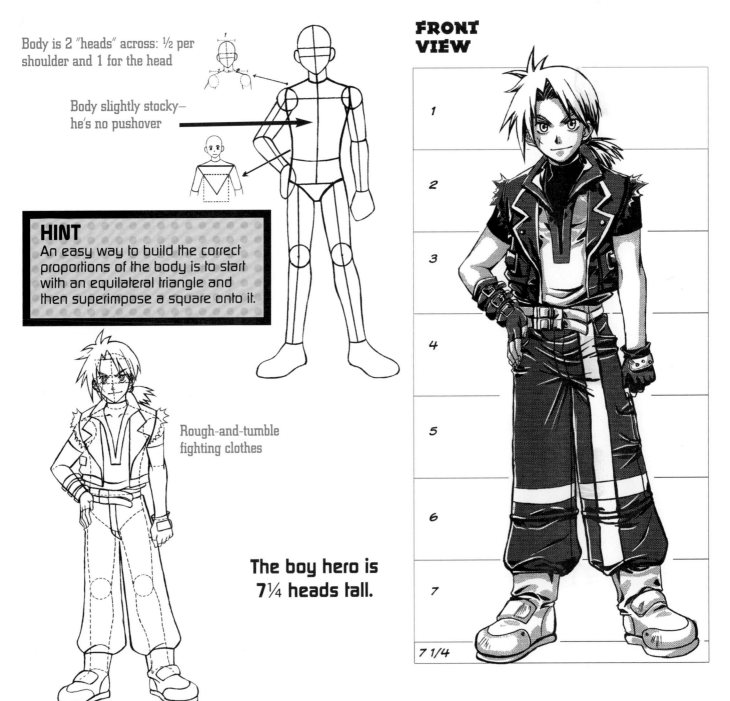

Body is 2 "heads" across: ½ per shoulder and 1 for the head

Body slightly stocky— he's no pushover

HINT
An easy way to build the correct proportions of the body is to start with an equilateral triangle and then superimpose a square onto it.

FRONT VIEW

Rough-and-tumble fighting clothes

The boy hero is 7¼ heads tall.

7 1/4

SIDE VIEW

	1
	2
	3
	4
	5
	6
	7
	7 1/4

HEAD'S UP

The method artists use to measure a character's height is to count heads. Simply measure the size of the head and count how many "heads" tall the figure is. Drawing horizontal lines behind the figure, as shown on these pages, makes it easy to do the math. Normal people measure about 6 heads tall, but our fighter boy is over 7 heads tall. Older teens and characters in their twenties can be taller still.

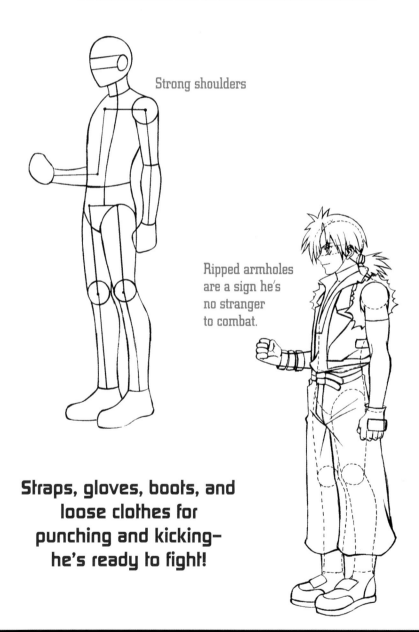

Strong shoulders

Ripped armholes are a sign he's no stranger to combat.

Straps, gloves, boots, and loose clothes for punching and kicking— he's ready to fight!

FIGHTER GIRL

This perky character wears her heart on her sleeve. You always know where she stands on any matter, because she lets you know in no uncertain terms. Think of her as the girl next door who just happens to have amazing fighting skills. She has a feminine yet athletic figure.

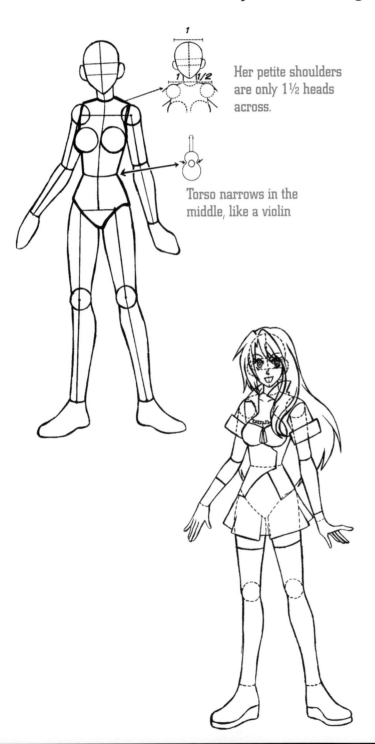

Her petite shoulders are only 1½ heads across.

Torso narrows in the middle, like a violin

FRONT VIEW

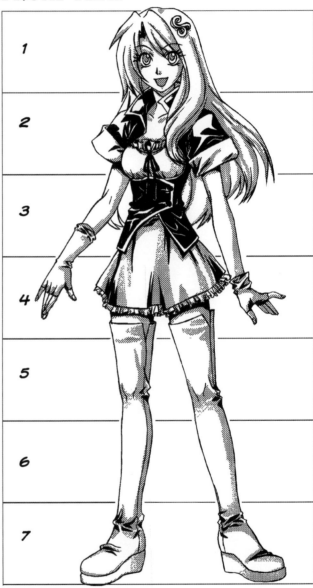

HINT
Tall boots or leggings combined with a short skirt is a popular look for teen girls in manga.

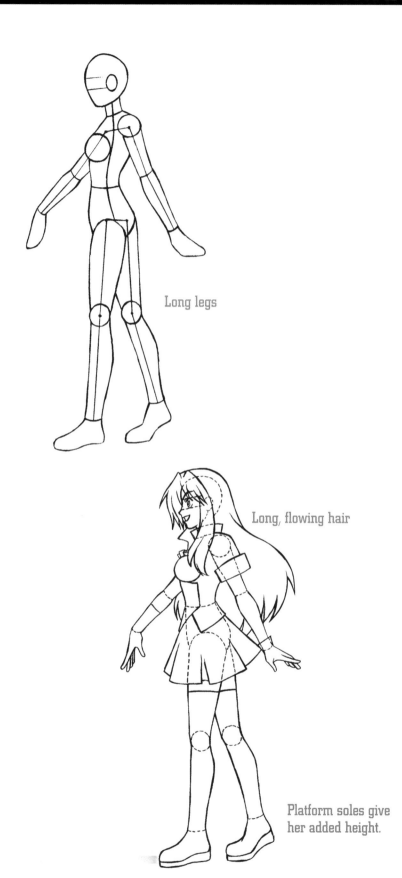

Long legs

Long, flowing hair

Platform soles give
her added height.

SIDE VIEW

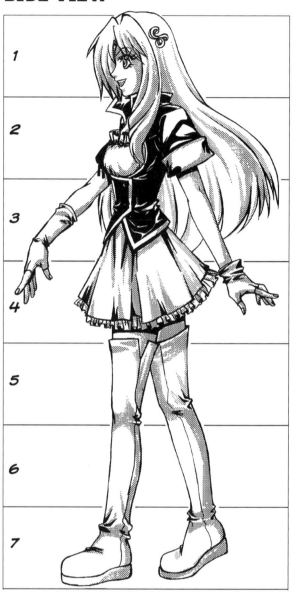

1
2
3
4
5
6
7

**The fighter girl measures
7 heads tall.**

Large head on short body

Cocky posture

Knee-length jacket

High boots

EVIL KID

Most people don't expect young kids to have the capacity for evil, but they've never seen a class full of kids torturing a substitute teacher! Kids who are bad to the core are great characters in anime. They're often tiny geniuses with terrible ambitions to rule the world.

KARATE GIRL

Pose, costume, expression. These are the three elements that separate the fighter girl from the passive "girl who believes in the hero." Her pose shows she's ready for action. Her costume shows she's a fighter—it's not casual clothing. And her expression shows intensity and courage.

Her stance, with her legs positioned far apart, signifies that she's not about to give up any territory. It's also a ready stance for throwing a karate punch.

Torso twisted to one side

Legs angled forward

Eyebrows crunch down in an intense expression

Karate-style "ready" position for punching

You want some of this?

ANIME ROBOTS

If you like futuristic weaponry and heavy-duty action, you're going to love this section. It's packed full of fearsome fighting machines, from colossal robots as big as buildings to smaller ones that pair up with humans. In Japan, there are artists who draw robots exclusively and are as skilled as architects, but you don't have to go to that extreme to draw yours effectively. In fact, this section will show you how to draw state-of-the-art robots no matter your level of ability.

Giant shoulder guards

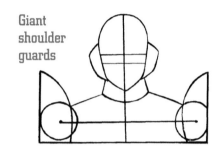

Form-fitting helmet

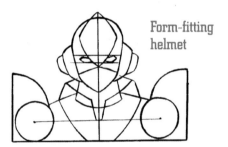

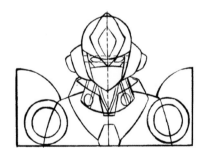

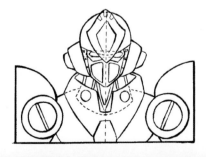

DRAWING THE ROBOT'S HEAD

Before we draw the entire robot, let's start off gradually by doing a close-up of the head.

FRONT VIEW

Because a robot is a mechanical device, it should be perfectly symmetrical in the front view—both sides have to align evenly with each other. This doesn't mean you have to actually measure the robot, but be sure to eyeball it carefully.

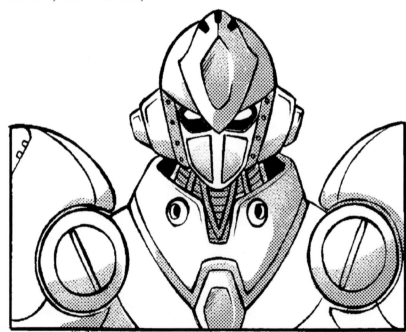

Many giant robots wear helmets and face guards that give them an emotionless expression. This makes them look programmed, and determined, to destroy.

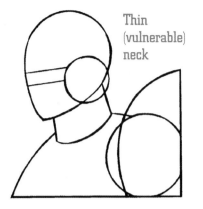

Thin (vulnerable) neck

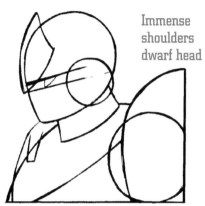

Immense shoulders dwarf head

PROFILE

The side view of the head begins with an egg shape, the same as on a human. But instead of adding features to it, add a protective visor and hardware. And while you should draw eye sockets, do not give the robot eyeballs. It's much eerier if the sockets are left empty!

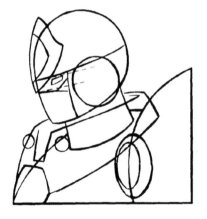

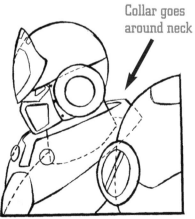

Collar goes around neck

The collar is large and surrounds the neck, which would otherwise be vulnerable to attack.

ROUND-TYPE ROBOT

Giant robots are built primarily in one of two ways: from box shapes or from round shapes (or cylinders). Let's start off with a round-shaped robot, because it's somewhat easier to draw.

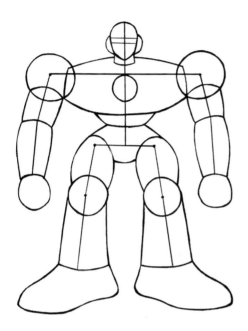

Basic figure is built like a human brute.

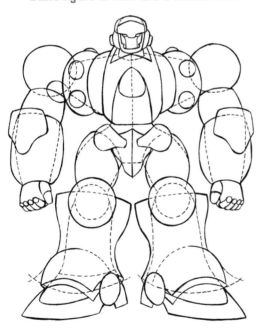

FRONT VIEW

Your first impression of the final robot might be that it looks challenging to draw, but if you look at it step by step, you'll see that it's actually not that complicated. Start off with the basic figure and then add armor to it to give it a mechanical look.

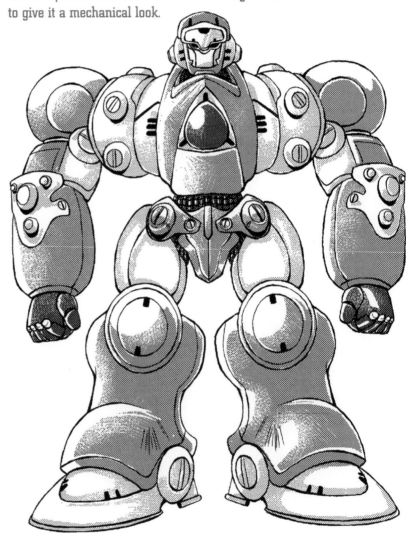

Note how immensely wide this robot is: His shoulders are spread far apart, giving him a super-broad appearance.

SIDE VIEW

If you're concerned that turning the robot sideways will make it appear too slender, don't be. This robot is so massive that there is no angle from which it doesn't look huge. The only three areas not oversized on the giant robot are his hands, head, waistline, and neck.

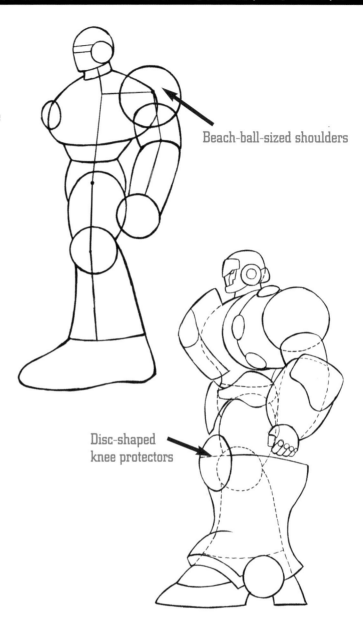

Beach-ball-sized shoulders

Disc-shaped knee protectors

Most robots have boot-type feet, with heels.

BACK TO BASICS

The trick to drawing a robot is getting the outline right. Don't start defining the gadgets and weapons until the final stages, though I know it's tempting. Once you have the initial figure in place, then you can add details.

You can personalize these robots any way you like. You may want to add your own style of shoulder guards, knee guards, and weapons. Or you may decide to omit some parts of the robots, such as the boot heels.

CLASSIC COLOSSAL ROBOT

If it's action you're looking for, it doesn't get much better than this gigantic, cylinder-type robot. Robots like this one are many stories tall and are usually commandeered by a human sitting in a cockpit inside their head. This robot's shape more closely resembles human anatomy than the other types of giant robots we'll see in the next few pages.

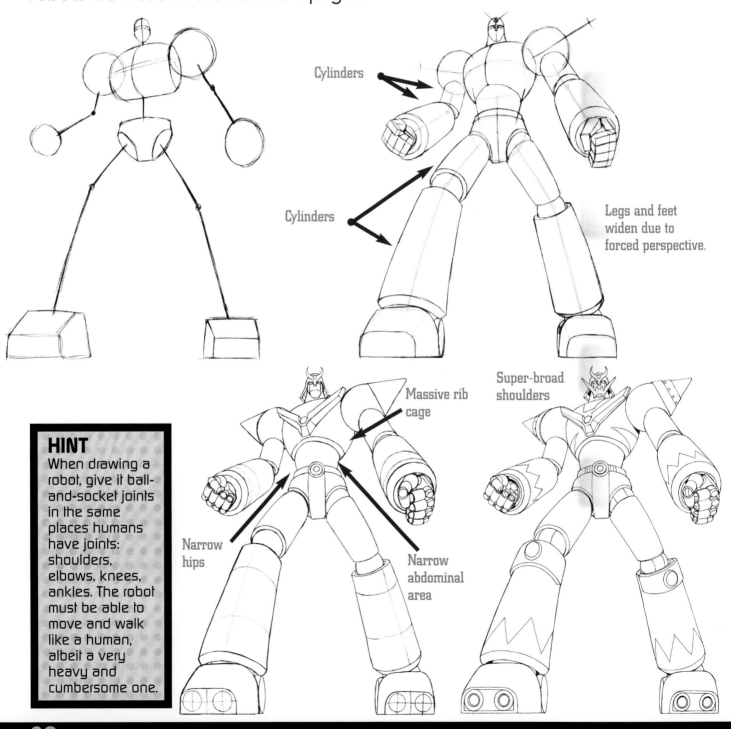

Cylinders

Cylinders

Legs and feet widen due to forced perspective.

Massive rib cage

Super-broad shoulders

Narrow hips

Narrow abdominal area

HINT
When drawing a robot, give it ball-and-socket joints in the same places humans have joints: shoulders, elbows, knees, ankles. The robot must be able to move and walk like a human, albeit a very heavy and cumbersome one.

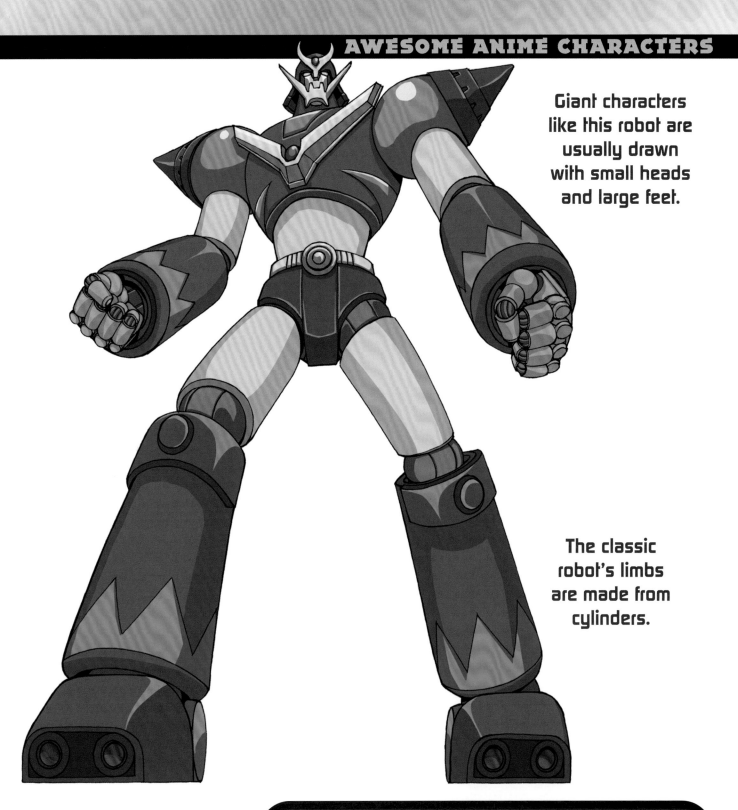

Giant characters like this robot are usually drawn with small heads and large feet.

The classic robot's limbs are made from cylinders.

KEEP IT SIMPLE

Rather than add tons of gizmos and technical doodads all over the finished robot—which is an impulse I understand well—put your efforts into creating an attractive pattern on the robot. It's more pleasing, and it helps the reader distinguish one shape from another. And it becomes the robot's signature costume.

ELEGANT BUT DEADLY ROBOT

This sleek bag of nuts and bolts is elegant, tall, and plenty evil-looking. But don't be fooled by the final image with all the fancy patterns and colors. A closer look at the first few steps will show you that this guy is pretty basic and easy to draw.

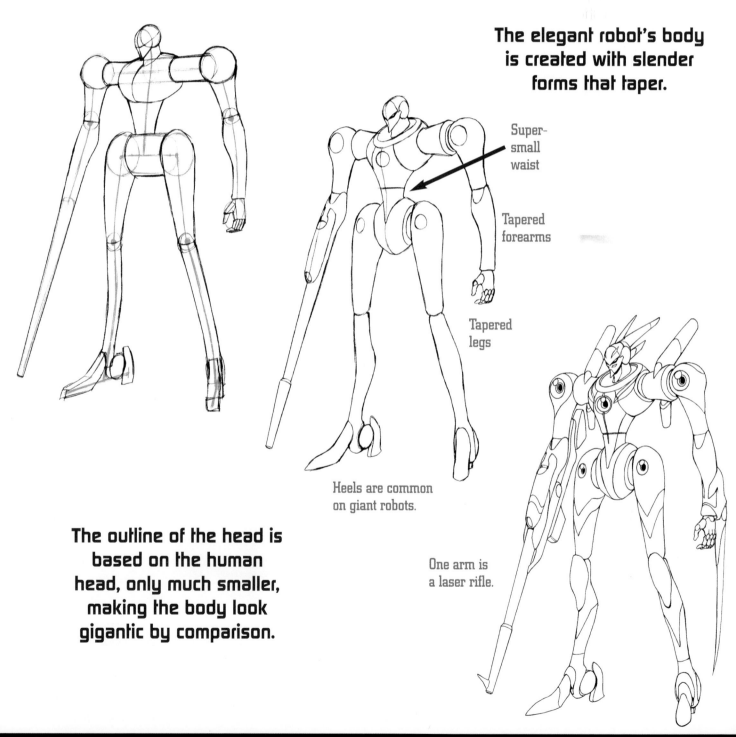

The elegant robot's body is created with slender forms that taper.

Super-small waist

Tapered forearms

Tapered legs

Heels are common on giant robots.

The outline of the head is based on the human head, only much smaller, making the body look gigantic by comparison.

One arm is a laser rifle.

TAKING IT TO EXTREMES

This robot's shoulders are actually wider than its torso is long. These are extreme proportions. Notice, too, that the arms and legs are constructed in such a way that it's impossible for them to move close together. This broad stance ensures that every pose will look powerful.

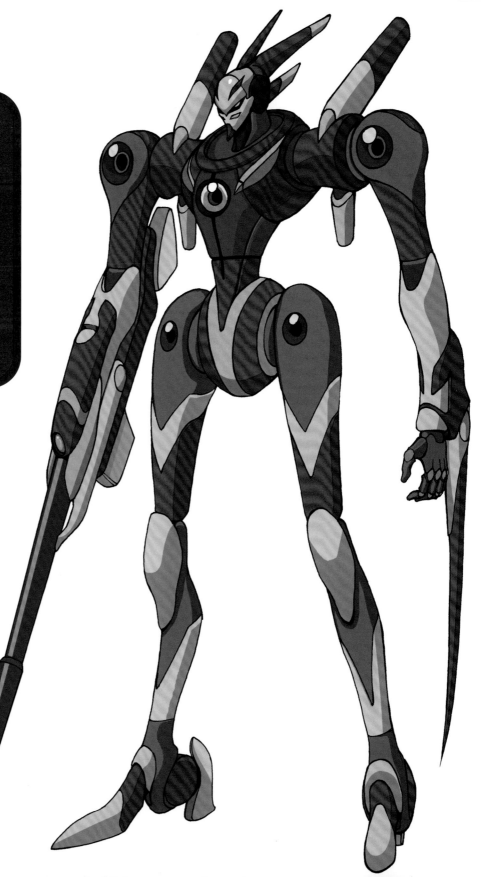

ATTACKING MECHA SOLDIER

Slightly leaner and more agile than the classic mecha fighter, the mecha soldier moves with more dexterity. Note how the narrow waist contributes to the overall slimmer look. This robot is built to get into the action quickly, react quickly, and take out as many enemy targets as possible.

MECHA SPACE FLIER

The mecha that are built to patrol the space stations orbiting the planet are hybrids. They function as ground warriors as well as space-based flying machines. Rockets on the shoulders and lower legs fire bursts like boosters, giving the robot extra thrust. It's effective to minimize the head and remove any traces of a face. All the design work goes into the flying capabilities.

ACTION TEAMS

Robots come in two varieties: the gargantuan robots we've been drawing so far and the somewhat smaller, sentient robots who work alongside their human buddies. Here are a few popular human-robot combos.

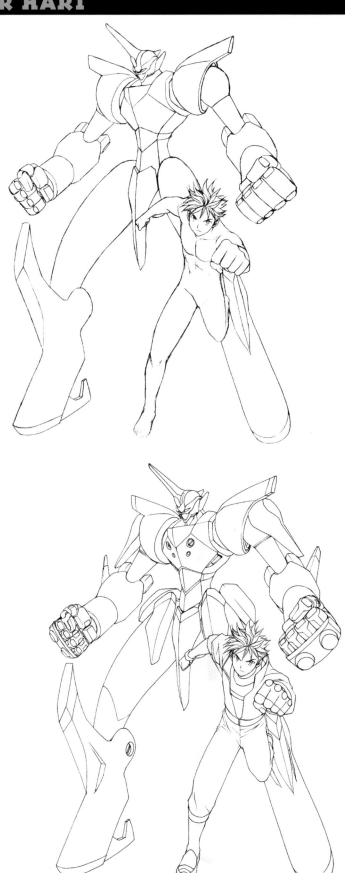

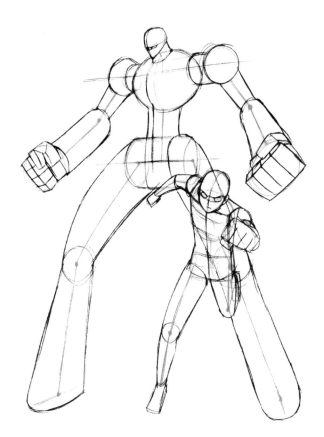

A BOY AND HIS ROBOT

This is a standard but *very* popular buddy team. The boy is definitely the brains behind the team, while the robot provides the enormous power.

VILLAINOUS ROBOT

Can a robot have a personality? Absolutely! Especially a robot of darkness! This evil machine communicates its bad intentions through its design. It is often skinny and lanky, with sharp fingers, pointy feet, and a brooding, darkly shining intensity.

The torso of this robot is divided into segments for greater flexibility.

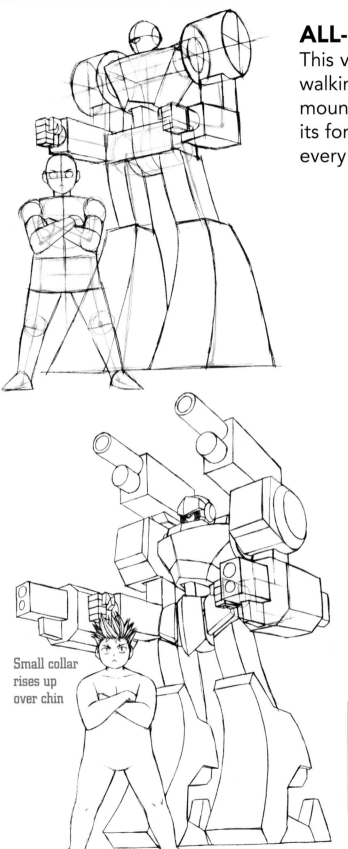

ALL-FIREPOWER ROBOT

This very popular type of robot is a walking weapons system. Cannons are mounted on its shoulders and guns on its forearms. It's the ultimate weapon for every young, evil mastermind.

Small collar rises up over chin

HINT
To make the robot look especially enormous, sink the head one third of the way down into the chest. The chest will look like a huge fortress.

This type of robot is very linear in design, with lots of hard angles, squares, and rectangles.

THE MECHA TEAM

When a robot is part of a team of human fighters, it's usually a good guy. One way to show that a robot is on the side of justice is to make it symmetrical. Symmetry gives the robot a look of stability and sturdiness.

Notice that the humans are positioned standing in front of the robot. This shows that they are brave and in charge. Remember, the robot is *their* backup.

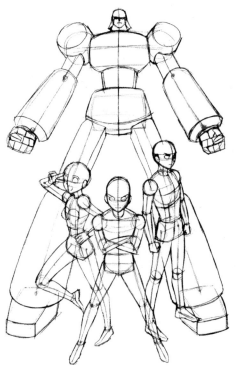

Give the robot extra-long shoulder flairs, for that "he-man" look.

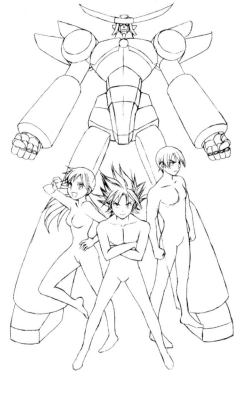